CW00690651

Colin Casserley first saw stock cars a
four years during the seventies and e
for turning up at the first ever Daily
in 1979, and his claim to fame is qu
meeting. His photographic collectio. .... 1968 – Dennis
Driscoll (274) was the first car he ever photographed.

Carl Hesketh first saw stock car racing when Blackburn Stadium
opened in 1978. Since then, apart from being a big fan and more
than a bit of an anorak, he has also been a scribe, a website guy,
a small-time sponsor, pit crew when times were desperate, and a
rubbish F1 driver.

Jordan Hollands first saw stock cars at the tender age of five and
has been hooked ever since. Currently studying his final year of
A-levels, Jordan's dream job is to become a sports journalist. After
writing a preview and report on the World Final, this is Jordan's first
published work.

Mick Jenkins has been a fan since 1969. A keen stock car historian,
he has written race reports for the local press and stock car
publications and is currently working on a book about Coventry
Stadium. He has never raced or been a mechanic but once helped
to push-start Nigel Whorton's car at Leicester – the car fired up and
Nigel ran over Mick's foot!

Rhosanna Jenkins is a scientist and current editor of
F1stockcars.com. Before joining the team she wrote a series of
articles on BriSCA for her university's online magazine which
were so popular they broke the website. So far, she hasn't broken
F1stockcars.com.

Scott Reeves is a freelance writer and publisher who, despite writing
several books on motorsport, is such an inept mechanic that he can
barely check the tyre pressures on his own car. He has been a keen
stock car fan since his first trip to Odsal Stadium in 1987.

Want to join the team? F1stockcars.com relies on volunteer writers
and photographers. Please contact us through Facebook or Twitter if
you want to get involved with oval racing's best fan website (in our
opinion!)

Published in the UK by Chequered Flag Publishing
PO Box 4669, Sheffield, S6 9ET
www.chequeredflagpublishing.co.uk

A CIP record for this book is available from the British Library

Printed in the EU by Print Group Sp. z o.o.

ISBN 978-1-9997774-1-8

Dedicated to the drivers who have left us this year. Race in peace.

CONTENTS

Tom Harris filled many headlines in the first half of the season –
some good, some bad

2017
THE YEAR IN REVIEW

New names on the track and new names on championship
trophies helped F1 cope with the loss of Coventry

Words: Rhosanna Jenkins
Photos: Colin Casserley

Like it or not, the loss of Coventry Stadium was one of the talking points of 2017, so let's begin on this sad note and get it out of the way. For many, the closure of Coventry left a cloud over the season. The internet was awash with comments; many fans thinking that the first Saturday of the month would never be the same again. Before the season started, there were still hopes that there could be a limited number of fixtures at the Midlands Mecca, but this never came to fruition. Not to be defeated, the Coventry Stox promoters took the show on the road, with fixtures at Sheffield in June, Belle Vue in October and Stoke in November. The battle over the Brandon site continues, with speedway and BriSCA fans both fighting for a future for the stadium. I've seen plenty of calls for fans to 'get over' the loss of Coventry, but this, as with any loss, takes time. The better the racing and entertainment at other tracks, the easier it will become to see a fixture list without Coventry included. That's not to say there hasn't been some great racing throughout 2017.

This year saw a first-time European and World Champion in the form of Nigel Green and a first-time World Cup winner in the Netherlands, Ryan Harrison. There was also a brand new UK Open Champion, Harry Steward. Harry is usually a mechanic for Todd and Murray Jones, but showed he can more than handle an F1 on track. Seventeen-year-old Harry hadn't even sat in the car before that week-

The UK Open was won by fresh-faced Harry Steward

Wimbledon saw a victorious farewell for Scotland's Paul Ford

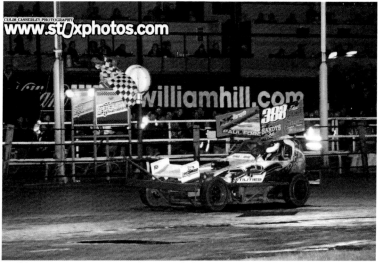

end but went on to win a heat and the UK Open Championship final. He'll definitely be one to watch in the future.

Also among the new drivers this year were Chris Alderson (380), John Fortune (164) and Drew Lammas (543). Drew Lammas was a name everyone learnt fairly early on in the season. Lammas took two Grand Nationals and one heat win before the end of April. Kelvin Hassell, on the other hand, was a name no one could seem to get right. The #13 driver appeared in a Newson hire car throughout 2017 and has been called every name beginning with 'K' (and one with an 'M') by various publications – including ours. Luckily, Kelvin takes this all in good spirits.

The season started with a farewell trip to Wimbledon in early March. The London venue hosted BriSCA F1 events annually between 1996 to 2007 but was set to finally close its doors at the end of March. Before that happened, 11 F1 drivers travelled down to London for a final blast around the capital's last remaining stock car venue. The poor turnout can be put down to the short notice and the distance required for most drivers to travel, but the select few present did not disappoint – the fence took a hammering and the track was torn up. Todd Jones and Mick Sworder provided much of the on-track action. Paul Ford was rewarded for his 14-hour round trip by winning the last final at Wimbledon. Ford then announced his retirement from the sport.

By the beginning of June, it was time for the first major championship. The British Championship, one of the rearranged Coventry Stox fixtures, was held at Sheffield and ended up being a record ninth British Championship victory for Frankie Wainman Junior.

Tensions appeared mid-season when some British drivers chose to travel to the Netherlands to compete at the Texel Speedweekend, which fell on the same weekend as the European Championship. Some drivers will always prefer dirt to tarmac, and who can blame them for that? As well as UK drivers heading across the Channel, there was a poor mainland attendance at the European Championship. Wesley Schaap was the only overseas driver to line up in the championship race and, as he failed to finish, the trophy for highest overseas finisher went back home again, unclaimed.

In an attempt to refresh the event, there was a change of format for this year's European Championship. For the past few years, the championship race had been a stand-alone race at the beginning of the Sunday programme. For 2017, the European Championship race was moved to the meeting final slot on Sunday and there were no automatic qualifiers. When the qualifying points were tallied up, Scott Davids found himself on pole, with Nigel Green beside him. Nigel Green stormed ahead to take his first F1 championship.

Craig Finnikin was among the rebels who raced in Europe rather than at the European

The Stoke semi-final meeting saw action, but not in the semi itself

In August, Venray attracted a bumper UK presence at the World Cup weekend. Ryan Harrison earned the right to sport the gold stripes, but there was also some impressive driving from the littlest Wainman. Frankie Wainman Junior Junior took a heat win and a fourth place in the World Cup race, whilst also setting the second-fastest lap of the weekend. It's easy to forget that the 555 driver is only 18 years old.

The semi-finals were, as usual, fairly quiet affairs, with Dan Johnson and Nigel Green taking the victories without much hassle. There was definitely some on-track 'action' at the second semi-final meeting though, which resulted in Tom Harris being banned for targeting Mick Sworder. Sworder later received a six-month racing ban for his team's behaviour towards the Harris crew. In one fell swoop, we'd lost two of the top drivers for the remainder of the season.

With the semi-finals out of the way, fans and drivers began counting down the days until the main event: the 2017 BriSCA F1 World Final. 2017 was only the second time that the championship had been held at Foxhall Stadium in Ipswich. The first was 2008, when Andy Smith led them off and was unchallenged until the flag. Four New Zealander contenders made the trip over: Jordan Dare, Wayne Hemi, Simon Joblin and Kerry Remnant. A good number of drivers from the Netherlands had made the trip across the channel; pre-meeting problems for Geert-Jan Keijzer bought Frank Wouters (H417) into the time trials as first reserve. Wouters went on to set the fastest lap and start on row three of the grid.

Everyone agreed that Nigel Green was the favourite to win it, and win it he did. Starting on pole, Green held back on the rolling lap, so his start caught Dan Johnson by surprise. He survived a caution and a last bend mega-lunge from Dan Johnson to take his first World Final victory. After Johnson's do-it-or-die manoeuvre, Ryan Harrison and Frankie Wainman Junior were left to complete the podium. Johan Catsburg was the highest overseas finisher in seventh, with Ron Kroonder also in the top ten. Green's good form continued the following day, when he picked up the World Masters trophy. Nigel Green had been the dominant force on tarmac all year.

After the World Final, all eyes went back to the Shootout, which had begun at Birmingham on 26 August. From the beginning, Stuart Smith Junior proved he was the man to beat. Ryan Harrison scored highly in some rounds, but non-attendance at others meant he could never truly be competitive for the silver. Nigel Green got off to a poor start in the first few rounds, so by the time he found his form again in the latter shootout stages, he was just too far behind. Smith closed the Shootout down in style at Belle Vue, taking two wins and showing off his new silver wing before the end of the meeting. It was

Lee Fairhurst blows some tyre smoke at the World Final meeting

Entertainer Rob Cowley's long F1 career ended in 2017

a well-deserved and comprehensive victory for a driver who had been on form all year.

The annual Gala night in mid-November doubled as a farewell meeting for veteran driver Rob Cowley. Rob has raced in F1s for forty years but is now hanging up his helmet. One of the sport's true entertainers, Rob made BriSCA history at Birmingham in 2015 when he became the oldest F1 final winner at the age of 63. A special race for Rob was part of the Gala programme and, strangely enough, the 73 driver came through for the win. We're sure to see Rob's face around the tracks in the future, supporting his son, Chris.

Overall, although the 2017 season felt somewhat subdued, that doesn't mean wasn't some great racing. The season hasn't been all about the loss of Coventry – there's been new drivers, new champions and, most importantly, some proper stock car racing.

What will 2018 hold? The provisional fixture list includes a visit to Mildenhall for the first time in quite a few years. Phoebe Wainman started taking to the track more in an F1 towards the tail end of the season, so 2018 might bring another regular female racer. Rule changes were also announced in late November, but it's too early to tell what impact these will have on car numbers. But with the rumours of shale at Northampton for the European Championship weekend, will car numbers be boosted? I guess we'll just have to wait and see!

Andy Smith claimed five World titles, including three on the trot — but is he one of our golden greats?

SIXTEEN GOLDEN GREATS

In over 60 years of stock car racing, over 5,000 meetings have been staged with over 4,000 drivers taking to the track. But who was the most successful? Ask that question to stock car fans and you'll end up in an argument about what that actually means. How is success measured? The most World titles? The most National Points titles? The most meeting finals? The most titles overall? Or some combination of all that?

Whichever way is chosen, the same names keep coming up. Leaving out emotion, opinion, personal preference; sticking to the cold, hard, indisputable facts, there are 16 drivers that have achieved something that the rest have not.

Words: Carl Hesketh
Photos: Colin Casserley (unless stated)

To date, only six drivers have won all three of the major championships – World, National Points, and British – and over 100 meeting
finals as well.

1 Stu Smith (1965-1986) Perhaps not surprisingly, Stu Smith was the
first driver to tick all the boxes. After a few years finding his feet and
learning to drive in a car that was a bit of a handful, a new self-built
car for the 1969 season saw him begin his reign at the top of the sport,
beginning with a grand slam of all three titles that year. His 100th
final came at Aycliffe on Sunday 19 September 1971. He went on to
dominate the sport for over a decade, winning a staggering 500 finals,
plus six World titles, 13 National Points titles and three British titles.
Mere statistics aside, he was revered by many as a legend of stock car
racing that will never be equalled.

199 Mike Close (1972-1987) A natural driver, Mike went from being a novice at the start of the 1972 season, to red top, to British
Champion in less than two years. But his driving ability was only
half the story – Mike Close was one of the sport's great innovators.
Both for himself and for others, he built some technically advanced
cars that had levels of traction and adjustment well beyond any other
of the time. Every competitive car in the 1980s had suspension fea-

Only ten drivers have ever reached 100 meeting final wins, so Stu
Smith's total of 500 is mind-blowing

John Lund's eight World titles is a F1 record; one which is likely to stand for many years to come

tures such as chassis wedge and weight jacking screws, all pioneered by Mike Close. He won his 100th final at Aycliffe on 27 April 1986 and retired the following year with a total of 109 to his name, but Close-built cars continued to win finals into the 1990s.

53 John Lund (1976-present) After over 40 years in active competition, he is now very much in the closing stages of his time as a stock car driver, but when he does finally hang up his helmet for good, John Lund can reflect on a racing career that is nothing short of outstanding. He made a reasonable start to his racing career, but in perhaps typical Lundy style he took his time getting to the top, hitting peak form in 1986, winning 13 finals. The following year he went even better, winning the British and the World with relative ease, and then the National Points by a massive margin. He went on to win plenty more. To date he has won 222 finals, the 100th on Sunday 6 August 1989 at Hednesford, one of his favourite tracks. His 200th came at the same venue on Sunday 2 September 2001 with a trademark last-bend hit. An interesting parallel between Stu Smith and John Lund is that both opened their accounts with a grand slam of all three titles the same year and then won their 100th final two years later.

55 Bert Finnikin (1972-1998, 2002-2003) A 16-year-old Bert Finnikin began racing in 1972. He made steady progress, getting to red top in 1977. A new car for 1982, with the combination of a Clive Lintern chassis, Alan Finnikin suspension and a Mike Huddart big block Chevy, took Bert to 12 finals and went so well that he decided to go for the National Points the following year. Although defending champion Mike Close was never far behind, Bert led the points from start to finish. The 1990 World Final saw Bert at the very peak of his career as he worked his way up the order with trademark cool and got the better of the then nearly untouchable John Lund. His landmark win came at Long Eaton on New Year's Day 1993, with the 100th of his 101 finals.

515 Frankie Wainman Junior (1987-present) He made his debut in a self-built car a few days after his 16th birthday and won his first race the following week. Thirty years later, you name it and he has won it – usually several times over. He is the only driver ever to win World titles in the UK, Holland, and New Zealand, and on multiple occasions in each country. Both a prolific race winner and a prolific car builder, FWJ has stamped his mark on the sport like nobody else. His 100th final was at Sheffield on Monday 25 May 1998, number 200 was at Skegness on Saturday 8 July 2006. To date, he has won 277

Racing is in the Finnikin blood – Bert can still be found wielding a spanner at son Craig's transporter

FWJ and Andy Smith spent years as rivals, but both qualify as golden greats

finals, and at the rate he's going, 300 isn't a question of 'if', but 'when'. Frankie is also one of four drivers to have won the grand slam of all three titles in the same year: Ellis Ford in 1965, Stuart Smith in 1969, John Lund in 1987 and FWJ in 2005.

391 Andy Smith (1993-2011) After a few years in V8 Hotstox, Andy Smith moved to F1 in 1993 and hit the ground running. He took his first final a couple of months later, his first World title in 1994, and his first National Points title in 1995. After a bit of a lean period (by his standards anyway) he was back at the top in 2000, taking his first British, and from then on he just seemed to get better and better. Finals and titles came thick and fast, including his 100th final on Sunday 20 March 2011 at his local Belle Vue. Andy won four of the five World Finals staged between 2006 and 2010 and made some of them look ridiculously easy. It seemed that nobody could touch him, but with five World titles, 106 finals and countless other accolades to his name, he decided to call it a day at the end of 2011.

Another six drivers have also completed the treble of winning all three major titles.

103 Johnny Brise (1954-1961) Of the many new drivers attracted to the sport when it was launched in 1954, Johnny Brise was one of the very few that had any prior racing experience. It was a big advantage, in terms of both race craft and car preparation. He began with a highly tuned Ford 68 Coupe before acquiring one of the cars shipped to England by the visiting American team in 1955, which he had noticed were fitted with certain after-market performance parts. His first final was at Oxford in March 1955, with many more following. He won the 1956 World Championship and the first ever National Points Championship the same year. For 1959 he built the car that forever dispelled the idea that stock cars were 'stock'. It took him to victory in the 1959 and 1960 World Finals. Having won everything on offer, including 48 finals, he left the sport for karting in 1961.

5 Doug Wardropper (1954-1967) Having worked on Merlin aircraft engines in WWII, Doug Wardropper came into stock car racing with technical knowledge and engineering expertise far in excess of anybody else on track. The ability to fit a 1950s Oldsmobile V8 engine

Johnny Brise's 1959 car redefined stock: a large Mercedes chassis, Ford truck rear axle mounted on custom made radius arms, front axle from a Fordson War Office Truck 2, custom-made propshaft, Jaguar gearbox, and 'as new' Oldsmobile Rocket engine (Photographer unknown)

Doug (5) and Alan (245) Wardropper parked in the pits (Photo: David Kipling)

into a 1930s Ford turned him into a final winner, before he took it a stage further in 1958 and built a new car. It looked like a Ford Popular, but hidden under the bodyshell were an array of carefully selected and assembled parts from a variety of sources. A winning combination, he won 26 finals and the National Points that year, but lessons were learned as the rest caught up, and it was with a smaller and much lighter car that Doug raced to victory in the 1962 World Final. He retired in 1967 having won 82 finals.

3 Ellis Ford (1956-1969) He achieved modest success with a series of second-hand cars that were already past their best, but it was the car that Ellis Ford built from scratch for the 1961 season that changed his fortunes. The car was modified every winter, such that by 1965 it was unrecognisable from the original. It was a revelation. Ellis won races wherever he went, and by the end of summer he had a massive lead in the National Points. Nobody got close in the World Final, and he won the British with similar ease. But as quickly as he had found top form, he lost it again, and the following season he won much less often. A brand new car was debuted at the 1967 World Final, fitted with imported racing parts such as adjustable torsion bar suspension, alloy wheels, and racing tyres. It was banned immediately, giving him the dubious honour of being the highest profile name to fall foul of the scrutineer. He won 56 finals before emigrating to the USA.

33 Peter Falding (1982-2007) The youngest ever World Champion, Peter was just 20 when he kept his cool to win a chaotic World Final at Coventry in 1986. He was once rated as one of the hardest drivers to ever get into an F1 stock car, but after a spell racing ASCAR on circuits, he returned a more tactical and considered driver, something that played a part in his 2003 and 2004 World Final victories. In contrast, his 1993 win was a total annihilation of the opposition, with pre-race favourites John Lund and Nigel Whorton just two of the many to feel the full force of the Falding front bumper. He retired in 2007 with 99 finals to his name and borrowed the Dan Johnson car and returned for the 2008 Christmas meeting at Belle Vue in a bid to take his 100th... but finished second.

55 Craig Finnikin (2000-present) After a few seasons in F2 in which he did particularly well on shale, Craig Finnikin stepped up to the big league with a self-built car that was not quite exactly like the rest. Never afraid to experiment with new ideas, it was with a brand new shale car featuring a complex rear suspension setup that Craig won his first final at King's Lynn in March 2004. He has been a regular winner ever since, and built a fair few innovative cars including the legendary 'tilter' with the body leaned over from the chassis. Although he has won on tarmac, he excels on shale. He's currently on 32 finals, 29 of

Peter Falding is the driver closest to passing the 100 final win barrier — will he be tempted to have another bash in the future?

SSJ started racing three years after Craig Finnikin, but he achieved the
grand slam of major titles two years earlier, in 2009

which were on the loose. He claimed the silver roof in 2011, won a
thriller of a British Championship the following year, and then gave a
stunning drive to win the 2014 World Final.

390 Stuart Smith Junior (2003-present) He made a big impression
in a one-off appearance in his brother's car, such that Stuart Smith
Junior made the switch from V8 Hotstox and built an F1. His first
final came at Belle Vue in June 2003, not many months after his
debut, and not many years later he emerged victorious in the epic
2007 World Final. He's currently on 44 finals and, while almost all
drivers tend to mellow with age, Stuart appears to be more aggressive
now than when he first started. The most uncompromising driver currently racing, his take-no-prisoners approach has won him many fans.
He went to the final round of the 2017 National Points with a big
lead, needing only a few points to secure the title, but rather than play
it safe with some steady drives, he went all out and won both heats to
lift the silver a second time in fine style.

That leaves us with the following four drivers. They may not have won all three major titles, but they did win two, as well as over 100 finals.

38 Fred Mitchell (1954-1967) His win at Harringay on Saturday 28 September 1963 made Fred Mitchell the first driver to win 100 finals. He was also the first driver to have flashing orange lights on his roof, although this was just for show – it was well before the super-star grade was invented. He was nevertheless very much a superstar though; a larger-than-life character and flamboyant showman with a driving style to match. Relying solely on raw driving talent, rather than the tricked-up 'special' cars that were starting to appear, he won 115 finals, the 1957 National Points and two World titles, but he will be forever notorious for taking the leader out on the last bend of the 1964 World Final.

2 Willie Harrison (1954-1990) One of the longest-serving drivers ever, Willie was winning finals almost from the day he started. With two British titles already under his belt, he clocked up his 100th final at Blackburn on Thursday 31 May 1979. But the one he wanted was the World, and after countless years of trying, it finally came good in 1982. Willie gave a virtuoso performance, and as the laps ticked down the air was heavy with expectation, it felt as though every single person there wanted him to win. He remains one of the most popular winners. One of only three drivers ever to have a testimonial meeting, Willie retired in 1990 having won 119 finals.

396 Doug Cronshaw (1966-1981) Doug began with a couple of old and well-used cars before building his own in 1969. When he replaced the lightweight Pontiac engine in his second build with a bigger and heavier Chevy 454 and found it didn't corner as well as it used to, he learned a lot about weight distribution and balance, which led to him becoming a car builder of some note. A regular final winner, he won the World in 1971 and the British in 1976, after which he eased off to allow more time for business and family. He won his 100th final at Rochdale on Sunday 24 August 1980 before retiring the following year. But after building a car for John Toulson in 1987, he took it to Aycliffe for a pre-delivery test and won the final, taking his total to 112.

Frankie Wainman's long career saw him take gold and silver and 119
finals, but the British Championship eluded him

212 Frankie Wainman (1970-2007) He first appeared as a novice in 1970 in a self-built and not exactly attractive or competitive car, but Frankie was a quick learner and rapidly rose up the grades to become both a prolific race winner and car builder. He wasn't the first to build cars to order, but nobody before had done it in the volume that the Wainman stock car factory was churning them out. He emerged as the main rival to Stu Smith in the 1970s; a decisive move in the opening stages of the 1979 World Final gave him his only gold. He hit top form from 1984 to 1986 and won three successive National Points titles, but the British remained elusive. He went on to win 119 finals, the landmark 100th came at Northampton on Sunday 2 November 1986. His last meeting was his testimonial at Sheffield in November 2007.

There we have it – the Sixteen Golden Greats. There are some drivers whose omission from this feature may be a surprise to some, but the focus is on measurable achievements – major title and final wins:

Major Titles

	World	Nat Pts	British	Total
515 Frankie Wainman Jnr	3	13	9	**25**
1 Stu Smith	6	13	3	**22**
53 John Lund	8	6	6	**20**
391 Andy Smith	5	3	4	**12**
33 Peter Falding	4	1	1	**6**
103 Johnny Brise	3	1	1	**5**
38 Fred Mitchell	2	3	0	**5**
2 Paul Harrison	1	0	4	**5**
199 Mike Close	1	1	2	**4**
212 Frankie Wainman	1	3	0	**4**
318 Rob Speak	2	2	0	**4**
390 Stuart Smith Junior	1	2	1	**4**

All references to the National Points Championship refer to winning the silver roof. There have been several different ways of awarding this and a million debates about them, but the official line is that the silver roof is for the National Points Champion. This was determined by the National Points Championship from 1956 to 2001, the National Series from 2002 to 2008, and the Shoot Out from 2009 to 2017.

The reason that only the three major titles have been taken into account is that they have been around ever since the sport began, and every driver that has raced has had equal chance to win them. Other titles (for example the European, Champion of Champions, Supreme, Scottish and Long Track) have been held for a limited period only and therefore many drivers did not have the opportunity to contest them.

Finals wins

1	Stu Smith	500
515	Frankie Wainman Junior	277
53	John Lund	222
2	Willie Harrison	119
212	Frankie Wainman	119
38	Fred Mitchell	115
396	Doug Cronshaw	112
199	Mike Close	109
391	Andy Smith	106
55	Bert Finnikin	101
33	Peter Falding	99
190	Len Wolfenden	83
5	Doug Wardropper	82
306	Mick Noden	67
244	Jim Esau	65
2	Paul Harrison	63
422	Nigel Whorton	59
3	Ellis Ford	56
68	Trevor Frost	56
375	George Ansell	54
260	Dave Berresford	50
245	Alan Wardropper	50
103	Johnny Brise	47
304	Dave Mellor	47
42	Aubrey Leighton	47
100	Tony Neal	45
390	Stuart Smith Junior	44

Do you agree with our selection? Join the debate on Facebook and Twitter – you can find us at facebook.com/f1stockcars and @f1stockcars

FWJ: now nine-time British Champion

4 June 2017
Owlerton Stadium, Sheffield

BRITISH

CHAMPIONSHIP

1. FRANKIE WAINMAN JUNIOR (1)

2. Stuart Smith Junior (390)
3. Mat Newson (16)

4. Craig Finnikin (55) 5. Paul Hines (259)
6. Tom Harris (84) 7. Dan Johnson (4)
8. Karl Hawkins (175)

Words: Mick Jenkins
Photos: Colin Casserley

Forty-four F1s attended the 2017 British Championship on what started out as a warm and sunny afternoon. There were a few no-shows and a couple of extras and in all honesty, the Sheffield pits probably couldn't have coped with any more cars.

Surprise starter at the back of Heat One was Jake Walker 368 (F2 298) in the John Wright (348) car, which immediately scuppered my prediction that Wright would be the lower grade star of the meeting! I understand that Jake had not even sat in the car until Sunday morning which makes his performance on the day noteworthy in the extreme.

The format for the British makes it imperative that drivers score well in every heat to bag that all-important grid position but defending champion Frankie Wainman Junior (1) had said he would be happy with a third or fourth row start. He set about his defence of the title in the best possible way, racing into second place before the halfway mark and closing on leader Karl Hawkins (175) with five to run. Downgraded to yellow for June, Hawkins drove a brilliant race to withstand a last bend challenge from Wainman to take victory. Danny Wainman (212) came out best in a battle with Gilbank (21) and Fairhurst (217) for third while Walker finished his first F1 race in twelfth spot.

Heat 1 winner, Karl Hawkins

Early leader Richard Woods managed a 10th place finish in Heat 2; right behind Paul Hines

Heat Two saw Richard Woods (268) lead the way as pre-race favourites Tom Harris (84) and Stuart Smith (390) traded paint and places on the way to the front. Ricky Wilson (502) stuffed his car into the home straight fence, losing a wheel and bringing out the yellow flags. Woods was still in front at the restart with Hunter second but Dan Johnson (4) was capitalising on his red grade start and ran out a clear winner from Harris and Smith. Woods held on for a fine tenth place.

Heat Three raised the biggest field of cars so far with 23 on track, swelled by late arrival of cars 16, 462 and 463. Team Newson had broken down en-route from the Far East. Hawkins, from the back of the yellows, was looking for a repeat performance but the race came under caution early on. A four-car scrimmage on the back straight claimed 34, 169, 462 and 463. At the same time Smith (390) climbed over Fairhurst on the home straight, leaving 217 sideways and 390 out with a flat tyre. Brocksopp (338) did his car no good at all, piling into the fence on turn one, while Jason Eaton (448) also clobbered the fence and needed medical attention. All this on one lap!

Hawkins hit the front at the restart but Mat Newson was in no mood to hang about – he wasted no time in hitting any car in front and was soon up to third when another caution, this time for Luke

Dennis (192) who was in a dodgy position between turns 3 and 4. Hawkins 'anticipated' the restart but second-placed Neil Scothern (152) put in a challenge, taking over on turn four with Newson behind. Mat took the lead before the half-way with Gilbank and Wainman (212) trailing behind, chased by 217 and 463. With a handful of laps left Hawkins blew his outside rear tyre and pulled off, then returned to the track to salvage a place before deciding that ploughing up the Owlerton shale was not a good idea and retired to the infield. Frankie JJ finally came down off the fence, as it were, to record a good sixth place.

The wet track caught a few out in Heat Four, not least FWJ who backed it into turn one all on his own. Johnson and Harris made no such mistakes, the 84 car hitting the front before the Union Flag flew after disposing of Johnson, letting Will Hunter (220) into second. Harris proceeded to fence a wayward Frankie JJ on turn one, the 555 pilot eliciting a collective gasp from the first bend patrons as he drove across Harris's bow with two to run, the 84 car missing him by inches. Harris won to maintain an excellent average from Hunter while Johnson backed up his heat two win with a third place finish.

Harris was also out in the 17-car Heat Five along with Newson, an early caution for Smith (293), parked across the back straight bringing things to a stop. Woods led the restart from John Brown (134) until

Chris Brocksopp hit the turn 1 fence in Heat 3, damaging a fence post

Craig Finnikin and Stuart Smith Junior battling in Heat 6

Hawkins took over. The 175 car entered the first bend backwards, a victim of the wet track, handing the lead back to Woods with Newson incredibly already up to second. Another caution, this time for Fairhurst and Dan Clifford (363) on the home straight, gave the rain a chance to do its stuff before the restart with Woods still holding the lead. Harris applied the bumper to Newson but just couldn't get the better of the Norwich man who was in front before the half-way distance. Danny Wainman, Mr. Consistent, took his third, third place of the afternoon.

The rain set in for Heat Six with Russell Cooper going well out in front. Stuart Smith spun himself on turn three and 364 and 483 went hard into the wires on turn one, joined by Harrison (25) and Riley. A bout of waved yellows followed, Cooper still ahead at the 12-car restart. The track conditions made the race a bit of a lottery, a cheer erupting as Woodhull half spun, trapping FWJ. Cooper spun, handing the lead to Johnson, Finnikin put himself in the fence and then Johnson also about-faced with no help whatsoever, putting Woodhull in front. Wainman passed the 335 car for the lead only to back it into the fence on turn three under pressure from Johnson with three to run. Johnson kept it pointing in the right direction over the remaining laps to take the win from Smith and Wainman who almost threw it away again on turn one near the end.

When the smoke had cleared from the BSCDA abacus, Johnson found himself on pole for the British Championship Final alongside Newson with Harris and Wainman (212) on row two. Row three comprised FWJ and Finnikin ahead of Hunter and Smith. The rain had stopped, the sun was shining and after a lap behind the water cart the race was on. The soggy outside line saw Newson lose several spots before he had even crossed the start line as Johnson led the charge into the first bend, chased by Harris and FWJ. Harris leaned on 4 coming off turn two to take the lead down the back straight while Smith repeated his spinning out routine.

Harris pulled out a massive lead, tapping backmarkers wide to maintain his half-lap lead over Wainman until he came up behind a lap down Johnson. Dan was clearly after a place in Team GB and decided to show Guy Parker his blocking skills around turns one and two. Harris continued to push the number 4 car down the back straight, Wainman closed up and joined in before Harris again made the break. A caution then brought things to a climax.

Harris led the restart with FWJ on his back bumper, followed by Gilbank, with Smith not so very far behind. Gilbank drove into the pit bend fence as Wainman chased Harris down, the returning 21 car delaying Harris enough for FWJ to line up the 84 rear bumper and send him flying into the turn one wires. Harris somehow bounced

Wainman took the lead but Harris survived to finish sixth

Passing the chequered flag to earn the chequered roof

out and continued but Wainman was in control although we had only reached halfway.

Newson ran second but Smith was catching him. FWJ was delayed by Dennis (192) allowing Smith to narrow the gap but he had the Johnson car as a cushion and crossed the line to claim his ninth British title. Smith came home second from Newson who must have been cursing his outside line start position.

It was certainly a race to get the fans talking with emotions running high long after the chequered flag had fallen.

Racing for Dave Leonard, the much-missed fan who was the driving
force behind the remarkably successful Under 25 Championship
(Photo: Colin Casserley)

WHEN FANPOWER
MEETS HORSEPOWER

Formula 1 stock cars drivers are lucky to perform in front of
some of the most dedicated fans, many of whom have given up
their time and money to better the sport.

Words: Carl Hesketh
Photos: As credited

Since the very beginning, the fans have been a fundamental part of stock car racing. After all, if nobody had turned up to watch at that very first meeting at New Cross Stadium in 1954, then the sport would have never got off the ground.

But it wasn't long before just going along to watch wasn't enough for some fans, and they began to get more involved in the sport. Fan clubs began to appear in the early 1960s and were either localised to an area or track, or were for a specific driver. By the mid-1970s there dozens, but today the only one still around is BOSS. The Bradford Odsal Stock Car Supporters Club is still going strong with an annual track championship and social event, despite the track itself closing in 1997.

The Fan Club Derby meetings were a fun occasion and began with the cars in 'fancy dress', being made up to look like something else, and with the driver and accompanying team in costumes to match. The first one took place at Harringay in 1965, and they were a regular annual feature of the fixture list for over a decade.

Yet it was the advent of the internet that brought the sport together like never before, with online communities such as Opposite Lock, Stoxnet and Allstox being instrumental in forming online friendships that often turned into real-life ones. In 2004, a collective effort by a group of fans made it possible to keep up with race results as the

The 212 fan club was one of many during the seventies
(Photo: Colin Casserley/Carl Hesketh)

Tony Neal's car in fancy dress for the fan club derby

meeting was taking place. Someone trackside would text the results to someone who posted them on Stoxnet. The first ever results team was Ales texting and Pizzastud posting. Those were their usernames: Ales was Ailsa Haigh; Pizzastud was Jane Redford, wife of Pete, hence 'Pete's a stud'!

Pete Redford's stud credentials are probably better suited to an altogether different kind of book, but he was the first to use the new-found power of the internet to bring fans together in the form of a fan-funded race. Fans donated towards the prize fund and could then nominate a lower-grade driver to enter. It was named the Internet Fans Challenge Trophy, with 380 Steve Cayzer winning at the Golden Jubilee Celebration meeting at Belle Vue on Monday 30 August 2004.

This was followed later the same year by the first Ladies Charity Race, organised by Kay Blackburn. Charities that have benefitted from the monies raised include the Drivers' Trust Fund, Cancer Research and St John's Ambulance.

"The race has been held intermittently for quite a few years now and is a good way of raising money for charity and for the drivers to give a little something back to the long-suffering ladies in their lives!" explains Kay. "On the whole, a lot of fun has been had by the ladies that have taken part and it gives them a little insight in to how difficult it can actually be out on track. You feel like you're absolutely flying when you're out there, but the video evidence shows things a little bit differently!"

Also making the most of collective fan power was Steve Cording. Rather than setting up another fan-organised, fan-funded race, Steve's brainwave was the Fans Tyre Fund. A donation to the fund got you a vote, and the driver with the most votes each month was presented with a brand new tyre, bought from the fund.

The idea was revived by the Talkin Stox group on Facebook, with the added twist that the driver receiving the tyre took part in a live Facebook interview – questions were posted by members of the group and answered in real time by the driver one evening, the then World Champion Lee Fairhurst being the first. About 30 tyres were donated in total, plus a replacement car for Tim Warwick.

But by far the most successful of all fan-powered events is the Under 25 Championship, devised by Dave Leonard. Dave had noticed that in speedway there was a championship for riders aged under 25, and with so many drivers registered in that age group he thought it could work in stock cars. The idea was a normal graded start but with the drivers lined up within grades in age order, youngest first. With help from promoter Steve Rees, the inaugural race was staged at Belle Vue on August Bank Holiday Monday 2006. The prize fund was made up entirely by donations from fans, all orchestrated via Stoxnet.

Contributors to the Internet Fans Challenge Trophy gather at the presentation

Rubber accepts some rubber from the Talkin Stox tyre fund
(Photo: Andy Leivers)

Dave's initial goal was a quite modest £10 per lap for the race leader, plus awards for the top three finishers, and that was achieved easily.

It was such a success that Dave ran it again the following year, this time at Northampton, but otherwise with the same arrangements. In 2008 Dave pulled off something of a coup and arranged for the race to be held at the World Final meeting. This time the sponsorship and funding changed with fans selecting where they wanted their donation to go, with various awards such as the driver in a certain place on a certain lap, the highest place of a particular grade, or the first car to be towed off by a tractor. It wasn't just money, either. Items such as tyres, vouchers, and crates of beer were now included in the prizes. The volume and value of the donations have increased year on year, making the U25 prize fund one of the biggest of the year.

In 2015, the event was organised somewhat at the last minute for the end of season gala meeting, but in only four weeks Dave still raised £2,500 and got together a 31-car grid. It was such a success that it has been held at the gala ever since. But, with plans for the 2016 event well underway, the event and the wider sport was rocked by Dave's sudden death. A larger-than-life character, he was well known around the raceways; his contribution to the sport had begun long before the Under 25 Championship. In addition to a stint as an F2 driver he had sponsored quite a few drivers. Dave's friend Lee Lawrence stepped in to make sure the race went ahead.

"After Dave passed away there wasn't a lot of time to sort things out for that year's race," explains Lee. "We didn't even know if we would get permission to do it at all. Thankfully we did, but things didn't go quite to plan with the payment schedule."

The 2017 staging was the first time that Lee had organised the race single-handedly. It wasn't easy, as he explains.

"This time around I was able to give it a lot of extra thought so the money would be split more evenly. Once I knew the drivers who were eligible I tried to find how many are likely to be racing on the night so I could adjust the fund as necessary. I've been told I worry too much, but I'm proud to be involved in what Dave started. I want to do the best I can in his memory, which is not always easy when money doesn't seem to add up no matter how many times I count it, or miss somebody's payment off the list, or get told money has been given to somebody else when it's not. Then when things are being changed at the eleventh hour it does become quite a stressful time! I know Dave knew it would be successful, and he gave it everything to make it what it is today. Sadly he's not here to see just how big it has got in the past two years. Dave never asked anybody for money, they went to him."

Dan Squire, winner of the first Under 25 Championship, recieves his trophy from Dave Leonard

2017 Under 25 Champion Lee Fairhurst with other prize fund winners
and a selection of prizes (Photo: Colin Casserley)

And the future? "Just to carry on being involved," Lee says, "and run it as it's always been with no significant changes apart from the three-meeting minimum and the change to 20 laps. One thing I can't be sure of is that the amount raised will keep increasing. I was shocked by the total this year. I know last year everybody wanted to contribute and it's not been quite as easy this time around but I have other ideas for fund raising. I'm not in it for the credit or making it bigger. It's about the race carrying on."

All of the above, from running a fan club, to organising a social, to raising thousands of pounds worth of sponsorship, was all done by fans in their own time and often at personal expense. It was done for nothing other than wanting to make a contribution. Formula 1 stock car racing is in a lucky position that is often overlooked – fans are an integral part of the sport, and without them it would be much poorer.

Stu Junior discovers an unknown story or two about his dad, while
Frankie Junior gets to work signing copies of his own book
(Photos: Colin Casserley and Scott Reeves)

BOOK
REVIEWS

It has been a golden year for stock car literature, with two legends of the sport getting their lives in print.

Words: Carl Hesketh and Rhosanna Jenkins
Photos: As stated

Overalls Off
by Stuart Milnes

This is so much more than a behind the scenes view of the career of the man widely regarded as the greatest stock car driver ever. Stu Smith's achievements have already been extensively documented over the years, and instead of the racing being the focus, this book is a revealing insight into the man himself.

Told in chronological order, the story is of a young boy with a difficult relationship with his father, growing up from a timid child into a flamboyant showman.

To the casual observer at stock car meetings, Stu Smith was confident, brash, and at times unashamedly arrogant. But away from the tracks he became a man struggling with internal turmoil; obsession and addiction eventually leading him to a life of hedonism, immorality, and occasional criminal activity.

While there's certainly some dark periods in the book, they are more than balanced by some lighter moments. Nothing quite sums up Britain in the 1970s and 1980s like speedboats and topless models, and both are mentioned numerous times. Other highlights are the late night visit to what's best described as a drive-by Bedford TK gear-

Overalls Off delves into Smith's life on and off the track, including his early years alongside Doug Cronshaw (Photo: Colin Casserley)

box replacement centre, and the reason why Stu paid a lot of money for an old Austin Allegro.

Written by Smith's friend and former team member Stuart Milnes, the book is interspersed with Milnes' own personal anecdotes, along with plenty of other gems collected during what must have been some fairly exhaustive research.

Whatever your opinion of Stu Smith, this book will probably change it slightly. A great read for any stock car fan, past or present.

Overalls Off is £20 and is available direct from the author. More information at teamsmithmotorsport.co.uk/overalls-off-available-now.

FWJ
by Frankie Wainman Junior

There can't be a stock car fan out there who hasn't heard the name Frankie Wainman Junior. He's won all of the biggest titles in the UK, the Netherlands and New Zealand. Nobody's won more British or National Points' titles than him. He was even one of the stars of BBC TV series *Gears and Tears* which followed the rivalry between the Wainmans and the Smiths during the 2009 season. Not to mention all the cars he's built for other drivers that have powered them towards the chequered flag.

Throughout the 30 years he's been in the sport, he's definitely shown that he's the winningest (to borrow a NASCAR-ism) BriSCA F1 driver around the tracks today – and it turns out our reigning World Champion is quite the engaging writer too!

Officially released at the World Final, his new book, *FWJ: My Life in Formula 1 Stock Cars*, is an honest and incredibly charming account of his career to date and his life behind the wheel. Starting with a foreword by former rival Rob Speak, the book covers the highs and lows of Frankie's whole life in racing, right up to his British Championship victory at Sheffield in June.

This is the latest from Chequered Flag Publishing, the company which brought you books about stock car legends John Lund and Paul Harrison, as well as our very own *F1Stockcars.com Season Review*.

Each chapter begins with Frankie's own recollections of different big races throughout his career. If you were there to witness them at the time, reading his accounts will take you straight back to the event. You'll laugh along with his amusing anecdotes – I wonder how many people in the world can say they've cut up an NZ superstock in an attempt to fit it within their flight's baggage allowance? And you may even get a lump in your throat when he's describing the tougher times – especially his account of the World Cup victory in 2015.

Throughout the book, Frankie praises the people – family, team, fans, sponsors and other drivers – who've helped him get where he is today. In doing so, he seems to capture what's special about the sport. They might all be rivals on track, but in the pits, it's a different story.

The book is a credit to Frankie, and to Scott Reeves, who not only published it but, in Frankie's words, helped put his 'thoughts and

memories on paper'. His dedication to, and love for, racing – whether it be his or that of his children – shines through.

When you start reading this, make sure you've got nothing else planned, because you won't want to put it down. It's written in a relaxed, friendly tone, as if he's just turned to face you in the pits to tell you a story – not that Frankie often has the time for that in between getting all those cars ready to race. Come to think of it, when did he find the time to write this?

Before you pick up the book and flick right to the end to check, don't worry, this book does not signal that Frankie will be throwing the proverbial towel in on racing. Yes, he's won at lot – well over 1,000 races in total – but as he says himself in the final chapter, he has much more winning left to do.

FWJ is a must for stock car fans.

FWJ costs £14.99 and is available from the Wainman transporter, Ed-Creations merchandise stall or online via Chequered Flag Publishing. More information at www.chequeredflagpublishing.co.uk/products/fwj.

The new European Champion auditions to become the next Stig

16 July 2017
Northampton International Raceway

EUROPEAN

CHAMPIONSHIP

1. NIGEL GREEN (445)

2. Ryan Harrison (197)
3. Shaun Webster (48)

4. Todd Jones (186) 5. Joff Gibson (249)
6. Lee Fairhurst (217) 7. Luke Davidson (464)
8. Ben Riley (422) 9. Michael Scriven (12)
10. Roger Bromiley (14)

Words: Mick Jenkins
Photos: Colin Casserley

The European Championship format had been revised for 2017 with all races up to and including Sunday's consolation counting towards grid positions for the main race. Some drivers opted to race on the dirt at Texel rather than Northampton and it must be the first time that a clashing meeting in another country has impacted on one in the UK, with at least three possible championship contenders 'going Dutch'. Scott Davids emerged as top points scorer on Saturday night ahead of Dan Johnson, Nigel Green and Frankie Wainman Junior, but several star names had some work to do on Sunday to improve their grid positions.

Alex Wass missed the Saturday night final, apparently due to gearbox failure in the 283 car. Brother Sam suffered major engine problems in his 284 machine so hard work by the Wass Motorsports team saw the 284 box relocated in time for Heat One on day two which raised 29 starters, racing under the two-thirds format. Martin Spiers (451), getting to grips with tarmac racing, led the early laps chased by Bromiley and Wass. Stuart Smith retired to the infield as Wass took the lead away from Spiers, the Evesham man sliding wide around turns three and four. Todd Jones (186) was soon up to second as Smith returned, then retired again but Wass was in command even though his lead was reduced by the chequered flag. Riley, Colliver and

Alex Wass took two wins over the weekend

The line up for the Championship race, with Scott Davids on pole

Ellis crossed the line three-wide to take the minor places but 'Wonderful Wass wins weekend double' would be my headline.

Nigel Green followed up his heat one fourth place with a strong second in Heat Two after a spirited drive by Richard Woods (268) saw him lead until the halfway mark when Shaun Webster (48) took over the hot spot. A repaired 37 car took third from FWJ, Johnson and Harrison (197) but credit to Woods who hung on in there to claim tenth, two spots ahead of Kyle Hassellhof (13).

Bromiley led Heat Three from Wass with Riley the first of the reds to show, while the likes of 1, 4, 84, 197 and 390 were slow to get going. Bromiley kept a tidy line despite being passed by Wass who was going for three heat wins but he reckoned without Jones (186) who applied just enough bumper at the right time to take the lead in the closing stages and carry on for the win. Wass second, Bromiley third and Scott Davids taking his first points of the afternoon in fourth.

When the weekend's points were tallied up, Davids found himself on pole for the European Championship Final alongside Green with Johnson and Wainman (1) on row two and Wesley Schaap and Alex van der Wass on row three. Under the previous graded start system Wass could have been a real shock contender for the title but the new format did him no favours, surrounded as he was by the top names in the sport.

Davids didn't just jump the start, he positively pole-vaulted it, crossing the line before the starter had found the green flag. Funny, I thought it was the starter who controlled the race but be that as it may, Scott led into turn one as Johnson sent Green wide but 445 held on in second until FWJ attacked, letting Johnson through for a lap before the gold top regained second place.

Green now made his move, whacking Johnson into Wainman on the pit bend, the number 1 car slamming into the fence and suffering race-ending damage to the rear corner while number 4 was terminally crocked. Green now had Davids in his sights but a caution was needed to move the stricken Wainman car. Controversially cars 37, 501 and H77 were removed from the grid for passing the pace car under caution, a kick in the teeth for Schaap in particular after making the effort to attend and the only overseas competitor in the race. Rant over – back to the action.

The restart saw Davids bring the field almost to a stop before he took off, again a tad early, with Green and Bromiley giving chase while Johnson dropped to sixth, slowed and pulled off. Green dealt with the leading blue top decisively, a big push into turn one followed by a dig in the nerf rail to minimise any chance of payback but the caution flags flew again to sort out a *ménage à trois* involving Frankie

The race ends for the World and defending European Champions

A happy top three: Green, Harrison and Webster

JJ, Whitwell and Whittle on turn four. Would Davids get a revenge
hit in on the restart?

To Green's relief the answer was no – he calmly drove away as
Davids fell victim to first Webster (48) then Bromiley, Harrison,
Smith, Harris and Jones. Another caution for Alex Wass, stranded
on the apex of turns one and two, gave hope to the likes of 48, 197,
390 and 84 but Green was in control, staying ahead of soon to be
second-placed Harrison as the race resumed. The action was taking
place further back as Todd Jones repaid Stuart Smith for an earlier
hit by planting 84, 217 and 390 into the pit bend fence in one brilliant move to take fourth, Harris spinning off the back straight and
colliding backwards with the parked Steward (512) car. Smith limped
around before retiring as Green drove a steady race, saving his tyres –
this is a twenty-five lap race remember – to stay a quarter lap ahead of
Harrison to record his first, but surely not his last major championship win in formula one.

Spectator numbers for the main event were certainly down this
year. Some of this could be due to predation by wild animals in the
long grass overnight, but joking apart there was something missing
from the whole Euro weekend, and I don't just mean coachloads of
vociferous Dutch supporters and mountains of empty beer cans. An-
swers on a postcard please – Europinion counts, or would do in an
ideal world.

Former F2 driver John Dowson Junior won four races in 2017 – Nigel
Green picked up a race win or two as well!

FROM F2
TO F1

Nigel Green's spectacular year has cast the spotlight on former
Formula 2 drivers shifting to the big league – but who else has
made the move and who might be next?

Words: Scott Reeves
Photos: Colin Casserley

In 1960, six years after the first ever stock car meeting at New Cross Stadium, oval motorsport reached a significant milestone. With the cost of racing stock cars growing – a familiar complaint even then – perhaps it was time for a new formula, one which could act as a budget, feeder class.

Under the leadership of Sid Farndon and Harry Twigg at Tamworth, the idea became reality. According to Stock Car Racing News, the stox newspaper of choice at the time, the new formula was designed to be "a nursery for would-be stock car drivers who could gain experience cheaper than is now possible". A few demonstration races – including one won by future F1 superstar Brian Powles – proved that the concept was workable, and before long tracks up and down the country were embracing the new Junior class. They were soon renamed Formula 2, with the Seniors becoming Formula 1.

Initially at least, the flow of drivers went the wrong way. Rather than the new formula providing a place where new drivers could cut their teeth before shifting to the big league, a few Formula 1 drivers downsized to the new class. Some of them were successful, most notably Roy Goodman. He had already been racing F1 for ten years before transferring to F2, where he won the first ever F2 World Final in 1963 and nine out of the first fourteen National Points titles.

Lee Fairhurst and Jacklyn Ellis, both former F2 pilots now plying their trade in F1

Rob Speak on course to retain the European title in 2001, his first stint as an F2-F1 convert

It took ten years for a big name to move the other way, from F2 to F1, and keep winning after doing so. That driver was Dave Chisholm, 1970 F2 World Champion, who became the bane of master F1 racer Stuart Smith in the mid-seventies, beating him in three consecutive World Finals (1973, 1974 and 1975) before injury forced him into premature retirement.

Chisholm was largely a one-off phenomenon and notable transfers between F2 and F1 went a little quiet until the new millennium, when Rob Speak decided to up sticks from Formula 2. "It had run its course and I wasn't enjoying it any more," Speak declares of his time in F2. "I suppose it was time for me to move on." In truth, Speak was so dominant in the junior formula – the 1990s saw him win eight World Finals and every single National Points title – that his shift to F1 was long overdue. If F2 really was supposed to be a feeder class, Speak should have moved up years earlier, but finance and the increased cost of running in Formula 1 was holding him back.

An offer to drive Jamie Davidson's car meant that Speak's F1 career became a reality and, once he did take the plunge, it didn't take Speak long to find his feet among the big boys. He followed Chisholm's example and became the second F2/F1 World Champion in 2001, adding two European titles too, before a period of retirement. Speak returned a decade later to win another World Final and become the first driver to win the National Points Championship in both formulae, in 2014.

Speak's second period in F1 coincided with something of a boom in F2 drivers shifting across. The next big name to join him was Mick Sworder, Formula 2 World Champion in 2007, who took the plunge in 2011. "I should have made the switch a lot earlier," Mick admits. Following him was a host of former F2 red tops including John Dowson Junior, Mark Sargent, Neil Hooper, Ashley England and Bobby Griffin. A two-time F2 Shootout Champion, Nigel Green, has been most successful of all of the new generation of converts, winning European and World titles in an amazing 2017.

This year alone has seen five former F2 World Champions take to the grid behind the wheel of an F1. Aside from Speak and Sworder, we've seen Daz Kitson (World Champion in 2000 and 2001), John Fortune (2010) and George MacMillan Junior (2014). The previous two years saw a number of promising drives from MacMillan's goldroof predecessor, James Rygor, who became F2 World Champion in an outstanding race that saw him start the final lap in fourth place but cross the finish line in first – and this after qualifying in the last-chance consolation.

F2 and F1 driver Mark Sargent will celebrate 25 years of racing in 2018, no doubt in his own unique style!

James Rygor lights up his tyres at Northampton in 2016

"I always wanted to have a go at Formula 1. It's the pinnacle of our sport," Rygor says. "Work and family commitments prevented me racing in 2017, but I want to come back as a competitive driver in the future."

What Rygor and his other F2 pilots have discovered is that Formula 1 requires a slightly different approach to racing. The vast horsepower of F1 means that races are often more strategic and technical compared to the full-throttle dash of Formula 2.

"I think it's harder to drive a Formula 2 car compared to a Formula 1, but with Formula 1 the racing is harder. Does that make sense?" says Jack Aldridge, the teen sensation in F2 who transferred to F1 around the same time as Rygor. "The speed between the two is different. The Formula 1 is actually slower, but there's often a lot more going on in races that you have to keep an eye on."

James Rygor agrees. "To drive a Formula 2 fast, you have to be more precise," he says, "but in the Formula 1 you have to hold your nerve more. You have to press the brake earlier – going slower is going faster, to some extent. The racecraft in Formula 1 is tougher."

Perhaps we shouldn't get carried away. Although plenty of top F2 drivers are testing the F1 waters, not many are able to match Nigel Green in taking the plunge full time. Rygor and Aldridge have been hampered by work commitments in 2017. Dowson is largely restricted to shale. Kitson, Fortune and MacMillan have only made occasional outings, with MacMillan's solitary appearance coming in the end-of-season gala at Birmingham. Few of the new F2 recruits have put in the 20 or more meetings each year that are needed to see them challenge for a red roof.

So what of the future? Hopefully James Rygor and Jack Aldridge will return from their stock car sabbaticals and put together a decent number of meetings to push them up the grading list, just as Nigel Green did a couple of years ago. Maybe one of the other former F2 racers will push on and start challenging for honours. There are others taking their first steps in F1 including Jacklyn Ellis and Drew Lammas, who have stepped up to the big league early on in their racing careers. Maybe they will end up as successful as another young F2-to-F1 convert, Lee Fairhurst.

And what of the other Formula 2 drivers who have yet to give Formula 1 a go? F2 is a national formula with 400 or so active drivers, of whom more than half can be classed as regulars on track. Who might be next to make the move?

The biggest name in Formula 2 at the moment is Gordon Moodie, a twelve-time National Points Champion who dominates the formula as comprehensively as Speak did in the nineties. Although he raced a few F1 meetings in the late 2000s, has he considered a permanent

Drew Lammas only began his F1 career at the 2016 gala meeting yet still qualified for the 2017 World Final

Rob Speak retired from the racetrack again in 2017, but will any current
F2 stars take his place?

move to the big league? What of his Scottish brethren, drivers like
Craig Wallace, Euan Millar and Robbie Dawson – can they be persuaded to leave the F2 heartland of Cowdenbeath and race south of
the border more often? Will F2 shale specialists like Daz Shaw, Sam
Wagner and Billy Webster be persuaded to take to the loose in an F1?
A superstar battle between Wagner and Wainman, Shaw and Smith –
that would be something to behold. And if Gordon Moodie joined in
too? Maybe even Rob Speak might come out of retirement!

Double World Champions

Dave Chisholm is considered to be one of the greatest Formula 1 stock car drivers in the history of the sport, despite a career that only lasted four full seasons. Perhaps it was the small matter of him winning the World Final in three of those seasons?

Arriving in the sport as the outgoing F2 World Champion in 1971, he was winning finals by the end of his first season. However, it was the purchase of a Doug Cronshaw-built machine from Stuart Smith that launched him into the elite class of drivers. Each of his three consecutive world final wins came at the expense of the man who had sold him the car, a fact that was not lost on the frustrated Maestro from Rochdale!

A back injury robbed the sport of the 252 pilot and we can only speculate on how many more achievements he would have to his name if he was able to continue. As it is, his name is written large in the history books as first driver to win the World Championship in both formulae and the first to win three consecutive F1 World titles.

Dave Chisholm – here driving the 252 heritage car in 2013 – was the first F2/F1 World Champion...

...26 years later, Rob Speak joined him as a two-formula World Champion. We're still waiting for the third!

Prior to racing in F1, **Rob Speak** spent a decade racing a Formula 2 stock car, where he racked up eleven National Points Championships in succession and eight World Championships in ten years.

Speak officially made the move to F1 in 1999, benefiting from the offer of a tarmac car from Jamie Davidson, who was taking some time away from racing. He found instant success in the Davidson car; winning both heat and final at Northampton in his first run out. The highlight of his first full season in F1 was winning the European Championship and in only his second full season, Speak won the coveted Formula 1 World Final – the second double World Champion.

Following a decade-long break from oval racing apart a few stints in bangers, Speak returned in 2013. After taking the silver roof at Sheffield in 2014, Rob Speak became the first driver to win the National Points title in both BriSCA F1 and F2. He followed up with another World Final in 2015 and another National Points title in 2016, together with a F2 British Championship win in 2013. Put it all together and Speak may well just be the best oval racer of all time.

Ryan Harrison bosses the Dutch in their own backyard

20 August 2017
Venray, Netherlands

WORLD

CUP

1. RYAN HARRISON (UK197)

2. Nigel Green (UK445)
3. Ron Kroonder (217)

4. Frankie Wainman Junior Junior (555) 5. Evert van den Berg (12)
6. Lee Fairhurst (UK217) 7. Peter Falding (33)
8. Roger Bromiley (UK14) 9. Johan Catsburg (99)
10. Frankie Wainman Junior (UK1)

Words: Scott Reeves
Photos: Colin Casserley

Due to inclement conditions, the usual time trials to decide overseas grid positions were dropped in favour of the average lap times during Saturday's meeting. Even so, there was no surprise to see tarmac sensation Nigel Green (UK445) as the top-qualifier, with Ryan Harrison (UK197) alongside. Yet neither were actually the best-placed Brit – that honour went to Peter Falding (33), who started in front of Harrison on the outside of the second row by virtue of being a Dutch-registered driver. A Falding win would really roll back the years, since he won the Long Track Championship at much-missed Baarlo in 1988, 1989 and 1992.

But it was not to be. Pole-sitter and defending champion Roy Maessen (400) led a perfect rolling lap, only to see the race stopped in its tracks after first-bend carnage left several cars stranded across the racing line. Second-time round, Maessen had to retire to the infield, leaving Frank Wouters (417) to lead the rolling lap from the unfamiliar position of the outside of the front row.

Wouters powered into the early lead from Evert van den Berg (12), while Ryan Harrison got the jump on Green and Falding for third. Then followed a typical Venray race: lots of fast, tidy laps, with the gaps between the front-runners increasing and decreasing by margins. Harrison nudged Wouters aside on lap six for the lead. Green found

Peter Fadling looked to relive his glory years, a quarter of a century after his last Long Track title

Harrison celebrates a successful invasion of the Netherlands with a few donuts

some hot laps to make up for lost time and took second place around lap fifteen, but catching Harrison was too much to ask.

Ron Kroonder (217) – almost as much a veteran as Falding – cruised from fourth row to a podium finish, but the most impressive performances were perhaps those of Frankie Wainman Junior Junior and Roger Bromiley, who made their way from the outside of the twelfth and sixteenth rows into fourth and eighth position at the chequered flag.

Harrison's World Cup debut could not have gone better, nor could the meeting for the Brits as a whole – eight out of ten races were won by drivers from this side of the Channel, with seven different drivers taking the honours.

Mat Newson's hire car business has become so successful in recent years – could we even make a grid of Newson racers?

FRIENDS IN
HIRE PLACES

Ever wanted to step off the terraces and get behind the wheel
of a Formula 1 stock car? One of the sport's superstars is giving
you the chance!

Words: Rhosanna Jenkins
Photos: Colin Casserley

Ever dreamed of getting into BriSCA F1 but don't have the budget to buy a car? Whether you have previous experience or are looking to hire a stock car for the first time, there is one man ready to help that happen.

Mat Newson builds, prepares and hires out F1 stock cars for a living. Newson's hire car business began when he offered to lend Luke Davidson a shale car for World Qualifying rounds a few years ago. After that, other drivers approached him, asking if they could borrow cars too. The business took off around five years ago and now Newson transports his fleet of hire cars to tracks most weekends. This is made even more impressive by the sheer distance that Newson has to travel. Based in Norfolk, Newson's closest track is King's Lynn, but he has long journeys ahead to get to the Midlands and northern venues. The hire car business provides some much-needed fuel money for Mat and his team and, by doing so, helps keep him on the track.

The hire cars require a lot of maintenance, which can keep Newson busy during the week. Sometimes he doesn't even get to work on his own cars until the morning of the day he will be racing them. The team, including Mat, his dad Robin and Chris Allen, works tirelessly on the fleet of hire cars. It's hard work, but they do it for the love of the sport.

Mat Newson congratulates Joe Gladden after a victory in one of his fleet

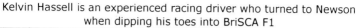

Kelvin Hassell is an experienced racing driver who turned to Newson when dipping his toes into BriSCA F1

Newson's dedication to the hire cars can put a strain on his own racing. Most fans would agree that he is overdue a championship win. Mat has 20 years of experience in oval racing (including six years in National Ministox). He's been on a major championship (World, British, European and National Points Shootout) podium seven times in the last five years, but never on the top step. He's also narrowly missed out on lesser championships, such as the UK Open and the Grand National Championship, although he did take the now defunct title of National Points Champion in 2014. Newson is considered by many to be the best current driver who has never won a major championship – always the bridesmaid, never the bride.

Yet those that have taken up the opportunity to hire cars are very happy that he offers the service. Nearly 40 drivers have hired Newson cars in the past two seasons alone. Some of the more regular Newson hire car drivers during 2017 were Kelvin Hassell (13), Matt Armstrong (455) and Wayne Marshall (483).

Kelvin Hassell, if that is his real name, is used to racing all sorts, but admits that F1s are a completely different beast. He's raced saloons, sprint cars, Late Models and Baby Grands (two-thirds scale replicas of NASCAR-style cars). Hassell made 13 appearances on the tarmac during 2017 and has nothing but praise for the hire cars. '[They] are competitive – I qualified for both the UK Open and the European in mine, and better people than me have won races in Mat's cars!' One of those people is Joe Gladden, who took his Newson hire car to victory lane at Skegness twice in July 2017. F2 driver Craig Tomblin (299) took a flag to flag consolation victory in his first meeting, driving a Newson hire car.

Matt Armstrong must be one of the few drivers who has further to travel than Newson himself. Armstrong lives in a village in the south-west of France. He had nine outings in a Newson car in 2017; appearing at nearly every track. Wayne Marshall raced on both surfaces too, making 10 appearances on shale and another 11 on tarmac.

So what about the practicalities? Newson charges £500 to use one of his hire cars, which is quite a bargain. The cars are allocated based on driver size – you'll probably get the car that fits you best. The race day procedure is the same as for the other drivers. Hire car drivers still sign in and 'go to tech like everyone else'.

Newson has previously said that, at meetings, his own cars come first, but in practice it's often a little different. He has been known to miss his own heat while repairing a hire car that sustained a lot of damage earlier on and needs to be back on track

Newson pilots one of his own hire cars to a win at Sheffield

American Eric Pollard impressed in a Newson car in 2014

for the consolation. 'Often the number 16 car is the last to get worked on, so those of us with a bit of stock car experience try to help out with the spanners where we can,' explains Hassell. 'Mat and his team work supremely hard to make sure all the cars are competitive and stay running all day.'

Newson has also built cars for other drivers. Early in 2017, Newson was so busy working on customer cars that his new shale car was not finished when he needed it. As well as maintaining the hire cars, Mat had built new cars for Paul Hines and Scott Davids during the closed season, and was forced to accept an offer to race the car he'd built for Mark Sargent when his own new car was not ready. Newson went on to win the meeting final at the April WCQR at Owlerton Stadium in Sheffield in the 326 machine.

Other notable Newson hire car drivers from recent years have included an American racer, Eric Pollard. He borrowed a car for the 2014 Coventry World Final and rolled it in spectacular fashion, coming to rest perched on top of the turn four fence. Pollard later moved back to the States, but was a valuable member of the team while in the UK. Pascal Spigt borrowed a Newson car for the 2017 World Final meeting at Ipswich. The Dutchman is no stranger to World Championships, but is usually more at home on the looser stuff. New Zealand stock car veteran Kerry Remnant also took to the track in a Newson car for the championship weekend. In the big race, despite starting towards the back of the grid, he made up a lot of places early on. After a couple of spins and a slowly deflating rear tyre, Kerry sadly only achieved a 23rd place finish, but was the only NZ driver to cross the finish line at all.

Newson hire cars seem to be a stepping stone for some stars of other formulae. John Englestone, a former saloon driver, ex-F2 man Jason Griffiths and former V8 driver Shane Geary have all taken to the oval in Newson machines. Former F2 driver Jacklyn Ellis hired a Newson car for her first year in F1 before buying her own car. Ellis told *Stock Car Magazine* that her trips out in the hire car helped her make the decision to move into the F1s permanently and get her own car. Jacklyn has also said that Mat and his team are incredibly welcoming and would encourage anyone thinking about it to have a go on track.

One day, maybe we'll see a Mat Newson hire-car only heat? Hassell explains that, off the track, 'there is some banter between the hire drivers but mostly we are all there to help each other out.' Running the hire cars has certainly provided the opportunity for Team Newson to make new friends.

Current hire car racer Joe Gladden chases down former hire car racer Jacklyn Ellis

Newson overtakes one of his hire car drivers on the Sheffield shale

So, if you've been inspired to make the trip to the other side of the fence, why not get in touch with Newson and unleash your inner BriSCA F1 driver?

Kelvin Hassell sums it up best: 'F1 doesn't really compare to any other type of motorsport. It's a spectacle and an art form all of its own. The balance between the intricacies of driving the vehicle fast and the ruthless application the front bumper is not as easy as the superstars of our sport make it look. I'm certainly finding it difficult! But I do love being out there. This is the best form of motorsport there is.' This happy customer has already given Newson a deposit for 2018, so hopefully we will see Kelvin on both shale and tarmac in the future, maybe even taking the chequered flag.

Thanks go to Kelvin Hassell and Anita Newson for their insights.

Mike Shirley poses with his immaculate Ron Rogers replica

ON THE HERITAGE TRAIL

Meet one of the men dedicated to preserving
the cars of yesteryear.

Words and Photos: Mick Jenkins

There's a saying that goes something like 'You can't know where you're going until you know where you've come from', and I have often thought that phrase could well be the mantra of the stock car heritage movement. It also summed up my situation one cold, frosty Saturday morning in November – I knew where I had come from (Rugby) and I knew where I was going (Mike Shirley's home near Meriden, a village renowned as the traditional centre of England), although I wasn't quite expecting to be travelling down Cornish-style single track lanes to reach my destination.

I first approached Mike at the Stoke semi-final meeting in August with a view to writing a feature on his latest creation, the Ron Rogers (152) car, but Keith Barber beat me to it (see the 2017 *Stock Car Magazine* Annual), however the offer of a private viewing of Mike's collection of heritage cars stood and was too good to turn down.

Formerly a mechanic for Bryan Warner (ex-90), Mike was a regular racer between 1976 and 1988, starting out with a former Rogers car, then going on to race a number of very neat, self-built cars which took him to star grade more than once, shunning the trend for Chevrolet engines by using Chrysler motive power. He sometimes misses being an active F1 driver but certainly doesn't miss the endless hours spent every night in the workshop fettling both stock car and transporter.

The heritage 152 debut at the Stoke semi in August

The Ellis Ford replica – a match for F1s on shale today?

Opportunities to see the heritage cars in action were few and far between last season, especially with the demise of Coventry, but there is no doubt that they are a popular addition to any meeting and always attract a crowd – witness the interest shown in them at Northampton in October and the Belle Vue Shootout finale last month. Mike has three F1 heritage cars, all of them familiar to regular fans, and the first one I was shown is probably the most well-known: the Ellis Ford (3) car.

Ellis Ford had business interests in Birmingham and Stratford-on-Avon and was the first man to win the triple of British, World and National Points titles, a feat he achieved in 1965. Mike's replica is a faithful reproduction of the car that brought Ellis so much success and is, I reckon, as fast as a modern day F1 around a shale track, even with its skinny tyres. In fact, Mike told me he once challenged Paul Harrison to a match race around Coventry but Frankie Wainman Senior advised Paul not to even try – he would never win! Based on an LD chassis, the engine in the gold topped car used to reside between the main rails of the Colin/Dave Taylor (135/136) 'Shark' car, while incredibly the gearbox and bellhousing came from the last stock car that Ford owned.

In the adjoining barn was the replica Jack Crawley (113) Raymond Way sponsored car, a 1947 Ford that Mike built up from a body and chassis found in the village. Way was a very successful used car dealer in Kilburn, London post war with a flair for advertising – "Don't delay – buy your car the Raymond Way" was one of his slogans – but he had been a fairground barker, Brooklands racer, RAF pilot, a boxing and wrestling promoter and a Lloyds underwriter amongst other occupations. I am surprised he didn't have stock car driver or promoter in his CV too, but his involvement appears to have been limited to sponsorship of Tony Rumfitt (13) and Crawley, both successful car dealers in their own right.

Mike told me the 113 car arrived on these shores in the same container as Duncan Bell's yellow Picture Post car. The rather crumpled state of the car is due to the fact that while the body (which had no doors at that stage) and chassis were stored in a field three large bales of hay fell on it, flattening the side. Undeterred, Mike repaired the body, found a flathead Ford, gearbox and axles and put the whole thing together. In one of those 'what a small world' moments, Mike went down to a hot rod and drag race show at Sandown Park earlier in the year and got speaking to a chap who turned out to be Terry Harris, a familiar name to old BriSCA/Scota stock car fans, who told him he used to work for Raymond Way Motors and now rents the old Way premises for his own business – that is until it is flattened for the HS2

Don't delay, race the Raymond Way – the 113 car at Belle Vue's Shootout finale

rail link sometime in the future. Keith Barber designed the sign job on the 113 replica – take a look at the superb Oldstox.com website for a picture of the original Crawley car. That was a 1939 Ford Deluxe, but Mike's lovingly restored motor is a fine homage to those old days when everything was black and white!

On now to the original reason for visiting Mike's Heritage Emporium, the Ron Rogers (152) replica. Mike has connections with the Rogers family going back many years: he remembers the days when Ron would stay overnight at the Shirley farm after a Coventry meeting before travelling on to a Sunday afternoon session at Brafield, Cadwell Park or maybe Snetterton. Mike was just a youngster at the time but Keith Barber's 'Time Traveller' piece in the *Stock Car* Annual answered a question I had been pondering – how did the Rogers and the Shirley families first get acquainted? It turns out that Mike's dad was brought up in Leek and went to the same school as Ron – another of those small world moments.

The fascinating history of the original car, from its construction in 1962 by Nev Hughes (69) to its last final win by Doug Cronshaw (396) no less in 1974 (yes, really) is expertly told by Mr Barber, who has been around stock car racing a little longer than me, but I do remember the 152 car scorching around Brandon in the late sixties.

Mike spent four or five years gathering the parts for the Rogers project, starting with a chassis from a farm trailer found by his brother-in-law Rex (or Wrecks) Hart (ex-167). If I remember correctly Rex was a silversmith way back when who crafted the Midlands Grand Classic trophy raced for annually at Long Eaton Stadium and featured a silver-plated con-rod from a Mick Noden engine – surely a 394 Oldsmobile – somebody out there will know for sure. After the chassis came the axles – an LD one for the rear mounted on underslung springs, just like they used to do, while the front one (Ford Model A) came from Street Rod fan in the village. The more I hear about the residents of Meriden the more I like it. The front axle is held in place by a pair of radius arms from a tractor – maybe not the way Nev Hughes did it, but they look the part.

Power comes from a 364ci Buick driving through a Buick gearbox of 1930s vintage while the Fiat Topolino body was supplied flat-packed by F2 heritage builder Chris Horner and took two months to put together. Working only from photographs, Mike measured the diminutive bodyshell and worked out the rest of the dimensions of the car from that. I reckon he has got the proportions about right and, as he says, there's not that many people around these days who remember the original. An ex-Army Humber steering box keeps the car pointed in the right direction while the home-made louvred bonnet kept Mike busy for many a long hour.

Stopping the bonnet from fraying is an Alvis grille supplied by Hoss Fernihough (ex-208 and sponsor of Ben Hurdman 207). I believe the original Hughes car featured a grille from a 1928 Delahaye fire engine, not the sort of thing you have lying about the workshop. Mike did track one down in Italy but couldn't get in touch with the seller. Having seen the price that Delahaye cars go for I suspect just a grille would cost a small fortune if you could find one, which I couldn't! Mike jacked up the completed car under the bellhousing to check the weight distribution, as Nev Hughes and mechanic Brian Powles had done with the original back in the early sixties, and found it to be pretty darn near perfect.

Mike has no plans to build any more heritage cars, saying he is quite happy to take the ones he has to shows and the occasional race meeting, but he has bought himself a new toy to play with – a 1943 Fordson truck intended for use as his stock car transporter. Called the Lively Lady, Mike reckons the truck was restored around 1984

Looking good for over 70 years old (not Mike, the Fordson!)

and remained in Surrey until 2003 when it was bought by a chap in Arley. He apparently never ran it and just stored it in a shed for 12 years. Mike couldn't see the old girl put out to grass so did a deal and became the new owner. I am no expert but the Lively Lady looks to be in superb condition and Mike tells me he has had the engine running – it's a flathead Ford by the way – and I look forward to seeing (and hearing) it at a show or meeting in 2018.

It just remains for me to thank Mike and wife Melanie for their hospitality. After viewing Mike's vehicle collection we decamped to the warmth of the Shirley kitchen where I was plied with tea, biscuits and stories of stock car days gone by. I really could have stayed for hours, in fact, I probably did!

Celebrating a third World Final win

16 September 2017
Foxhall Stadium, Ipswich

WORLD CHAMPIONSHIP

1. NIGEL GREEN (445)

2. Ryan Harrison (197)
3. Frankie Wainman Junior (1)

4. Stuart Smith Junior (390) 5. Rob Speak (318)
6. Johan Catsburg (H99) 7. Ron Kroonder (H217)
8. Luke Davidson (464) 9. Danny Wainman (212)
10. Mat Newson (16)

Words: Mick Jenkins
Photos: Colin Casserley

The pre-meeting time trials for the overseas competitors proved disastrous for one of Holland's top drivers, Geert-Jan Keijzer (H6), who sadly had major engine problems and was forced to load up, never turning a wheel in anger all weekend. A cruel stroke of luck but this brought in Frank Wouters (H417) as first reserve who went on to set the fastest lap and claim the inside row three berth alongside Wesley Schaap (H77).

The feeling prior to the 2017 World Final seemed to be that if pole sitter Nigel Green (445) cleared the first bend unscathed he would be uncatchable and so it proved to be.

Thirty-six cars took to the track, front men Green and Dan Johnson (4) setting a fast rolling lap before slowing at the end of the back straight. Instead of coming to the flag side by side, Green held back, a couple of car lengths behind Johnson and then floored it, catching Dan by surprise. The 445 car did indeed clear turn one unscathed, chased by Johnson, while Stuart Smith Junior (390) landed a big hit on Paul Hines (259).

The push came from further back, chief suspects being Rob Speak (318) or Mark Gilbank (21) and the overseas challenge ended there and then, with Wouters, Schaap, Jan Roelof Wijbenga (H228), Christiaan Weyenberg (H380) and Wayne Hemi (NZ591) all involved along with Gilbank and Davidson.

The cause of the caution – and the end of the race for many overseas drivers…

...and the resulting damage to NZ591

The loaned and superbly presented NZ591 car was severely damaged, with both outside wheels ripped off, one wheel making its own way down the back straight. The race was brought under caution, all drivers thankfully uninjured while the first bend car park was cleared.

The restart order top ten was 445, 4, (464), 1, 390, 197, 259, H217, 318, 55 and H99 with Johnson literally right on the 445 back bumper. At the green Nigel again shot away, backmarker Davidson moving aside to let the train of cars go through. Smith tried to remove defending champion Wainman but then came in for some attention from Ryan Harrison (197).

As Simon Joblin (NZ1) drifted onto the shale inner track (probably felt more at home there), Green, as expected began to pull away, putting several car lengths between himself and Johnson. Joblin returned to the tarmac, using the bumper to good effect and showing an impressive turn of speed as the leader encountered backmarkers. Moving inside Jan Kuin (H699), the Dutch dirt track driver became one of only two men to land a blow on the 445 car all race, whacking Green's back bumper as they charged into turn three before spinning out.

All this was allowing Johnson to close the gap on the leader, while Harrison took fourth off Smith. Green received another scare, this time from Evert van den Berg (H12) who clattered into the 445 rear bumper, sending him wide but he held on, sending Drew Lammas (543) wide on the next bend to clear a path then repaying Kuin on the next corner. A yellow flag raised on turn four for Jordan Dare (NZ2) went unheeded as Joblin spun on turn one ahead of leader Green.

Thoughts of history repeating itself dissolved as the Leicestershire man negotiated the bend successfully, keeping well ahead of Johnson. With five to run, Harrison passed Wainman for third who then came under attack from Smith but FWJ found a bit of extra speed to move clear. On the final lap, with no backmarkers between himself and Green, Johnson went for an outrageous last bender, jumping the kerb in a last ditch effort to remove the 445 car, missing and piling into the fence, never to finish. Green powered off the bend for victory with Harrison promoted to second and outgoing champion Wainman third.

Congratulations to Nigel Green who adds the World Championship to the European title he won in July with a cool, calculated drive. He came close to taking the silver roof last season – what are the odds on him going all the way this year?

As in the 2008 event this was a race for stock cars, not a stock car race. Very, very fast but, as with many World Finals, very little incident beyond the first bend pile-up. Talking of that first bend shunt,

Nigel Green might have avoided being bumpered, but there was plenty of action further down the grid

The top three escape the chilly air courtesy of the Ipswich flamethrowers

can I offer my apologies to New Zealander Wayne Hemi and Team Fairhurst for all the damage done to 'Trigger's Broom'. Wayne was the only driver at Ipswich I shook hands with and wished good luck for the big race. Commentator's curse is well known, but writer's curse?

SSJ takes the applause of his many fans after seizing the silver roof for the second time

STOX PERSONALITY OF THE YEAR

STUART SMITH JUNIOR

The Stox Personality of the Year was chosen by a public vote on the F1stockcars.com website in December 2017. Four drivers were shortlisted, chosen by the 2016 winner, Mick Sworder.

The other shortlisted personalities were:
Todd Jones
Harry Steward
Frankie Wainman Junior Junior

Previous winners of the award:
2016 Mick Sworder
2015 Frankie Wainman Junior

Words: Scott Reeves
Photos: Colin Casserley

"If someone wants to start a war, they can. But they will lose…"

That was the fighting talk coming from Stuart Smith Junior on the eve of the National Points Championship Shootout finale at Belle Vue. History records that nobody did want to start a war with him that day. Smith wrapped up the title that everybody already knew was his with two heat wins on the bounce. Such was Smith's determination to win the title in style that he attempted a risky last-bender on James Morris. And it worked. Everything came together perfectly and Smith won the Shootout for the second time, but it was the most comprehensive victory since the Shootout was dreamed up in 2009.

The joy that Smith felt at winning the Shootout was matched on the terraces too. Fans of the Rochdale Smiths have been starved of silverware for too long, but winning the silver roof – and the manner in which Stuart did it – seems to have rejuvenated them. There is talk of reviving the Zigger Zagger crew that used to chant the name of Stuart Senior, perhaps even setting up a modern-day fan club. That would be welcome. A bit of partisanship and friendly rivalry might bring a bit of colour back to the terraces, especially given the gloom that has pervaded since the Coventry debacle.

Everybody will remember Smith's run to silver, but don't forget that he won the final in two out of the first six meetings – admit-

2017 ranks as one of Smith's finest seasons behind the wheel, with major championship success the icing on the cake

Smith wrapped up the silver roof with two races to spare — quite an achievement considering the double points on offer at the finale

tedly starting from red grade, but making full use of the advantage — which saw him top the grading points after the first period. Although Frankie Wainman Junior and Nigel Green eventually elbowed their way past, Smith remained in the top three for the rest of the year.

His statistical achievements make impressive reading and signal a consistency that has been missing for the past few seasons. He had the second-highest points-per-meeting average (behind Green), second-highest number of shale points (behind Wainman), second-highest number of final wins (behind Green again), third-highest number of tarmac points (behind Green and Wainman), and the highest number of overall race wins (26 compared to Green's 22).

We caught up with SSJ shortly after the end of the season and asked him about his year behind the wheel:

It's been your best season for some time – have you done anything differently this year?

I have some really good lads behind me at the minute. That enabled me to be dedicated without sacrificing too much time away from work. It's all down to the team as a whole, the sponsors and the fans.

Why do you think nobody was able to challenge you for the National Points Shootout?

I have never blown up my own arse, I'm not like that, but I have always been one to beat. It's just that everything else has to be in the right place at the right time. What I mean by that is work, money, family, equipment team sponsors, etc... However, at this particular time I believe I have driven better than anyone else too!

www.stoxphotos.com

With 26 race wins, Stuart took the chequered flag more than any other driver in 2017

Aside from a stunning silver roof campaign, Smith is one of F1's most entertaining and skilled drivers

What's your approach to races?

To win at all costs within the spirit of the sport. That is what is great about the sport – we should race hard and never take it off track.

You're well known for being aggressive when the situation calls for it and you carved through the field like a man on a mission during the Shootout. Do you think other drivers are prepared to use the bumper enough?

I think everyone can use the bumper well. Some do it more calculated than others which seems go to under the radar, but everyone is willing to use it.

F1 fans will be hoping for this kind of action (from the 2016 F2 World Final) when the big league returns to Mildenhall

THE RETURN
OF MILDENHALL

Formula 1 stock car racing will return to the Suffolk shale in
2018 – but can Mildenhall fill the gaping void left by a certain
Midlands stadium?

Words: Jordan Hollands
Photos: Colin Casserley

After the sad demise of Coventry's Brandon Stadium at the end of 2016, many fans were left wondering which other shale-surfaced track would fill the void of such an iconic track. When the 2017 fixtures were announced, it seemed no other would replace Coventry, instead some meetings were renamed as part of the 'CoventryStox on Tour' schedule.

The result? Some drivers such as John Lund did not take to the track during the 2017 season. Was it due to the lambing season, work at the farm or injuries, or was it down to the 'Coventry effect'?

But with the proposed fixtures for the 2018 season being announced, that huge gap that Coventry left behind may now finally be filled. After rumours circulating all season long, it was announced that F1 stock cars will be making a welcome return to Mildenhall Stadium in 2018, on Saturday 7 April.

Most of the younger fans may not remember Mildenhall when it was an F1 track. The stadium was built back in 1971 as a speedway venue. Stock car racing was introduced in the early 1980s by promoter Vince Moody, who also promoted Skegness and Boston.

F1s made their debut in the 1987 season, but the seven meetings held there didn't get massive car turnouts or massive crowds, probably due to a combination of a remote location and the meetings being on a Sunday afternoon following either Crewe or Long Eaton, or on the same day as Aycliffe.

Mildenhall hosted the 2017 Saloon Stock Car European Championship

Will any Dutch drivers cross the Channel for the 2018 fixture?

For the following season, the number of meetings held at Mildenhall was reduced to just four, all of which were held on a Sunday afternoon. These meetings included a World Championship Qualifying Round, a Grand Prix round and the BriSCA Supreme Championship, but it still wasn't enough to get the crowd or cars at the Suffolk shale venue. And at the end of that season, it was dropped from the calendar.

After a 13-year absence, F1s returned to Mildenhall Stadium in 2002 as part of a King's Lynn and Mildenhall weekender to try to boost numbers of both spectators and drivers. Sadly though, the turn-out was the lowest for shale that year and Mildenhall was once again dropped from the F1 calendar. The final that day went the way of a local lad, 93 Steve Taylor, in what was his only ever F1 final win.

Although the 12 meetings held at Mildenhall resulted in low numbers of cars and attendance figures, the meetings normally provided some good action given the small technical layout of the track. Chris 'Smokey' Bimmell once even tried getting around the whole track without taking his foot off the gas, going sideways all the way!

The return of any shale track should be celebrated. After all, the phrase 'tarmac's for getting there, shale's for racing' appears to have come into fruition for a few drivers. A good example of this is the European Championship weekender held at Northampton International Raceway, which has struggled for numbers over the last couple of years. The European title has struggled to get Dutch drivers due to how popular the shale scene is in Holland in comparison to how poor the tarmac scene is. Because of this, many fans have suggested moving the European weekender to Mildenhall. That seems unlikely due to the small size of Mildenhall and, so many believe, a promoters' agreement that Northampton remains the home of the Euro weekender.

However, rumours developed late in 2017 suggesting that Northampton would be transformed into a shale track for the Euro weekend to try to entice the Dutch drivers back. It was confirmed in early December that Northampton would indeed be turned shale for the summer months, meaning the European weekend and World Masters would be raced on shale in 2018.

Yet despite the commonly accepted fact that most drivers prefer shale to tarmac, the average car attendance for tarmac during the 2017 season was 43.09 per meeting – actually better than the average car attendance for shale last season, which was 34.36 per meeting. That's quite an interesting statistic considering that shale is supposed to be the preferred surface. Maybe it was down to the World Final being on tarmac, or is it the impact of the dreaded 'Coventry effect'?

Andy Watts, the official commentator at Mildenhall Stadium, said, "I reckon next year's fixture will get mixed reactions. Some will

Only a few active drivers have raced F1s at Mildenhall, including FWJ...

...but perhaps the lower graders at the front will enjoy the tight track

be happy to race at Mildenhall as they haven't been there for many years and for many it would be their first time racing at Mildenhall in the formula." Andy added, "I would say it will get a lot of public interest as well, providing car numbers are good, but I also feel it may struggle due to the size of the track regarding the width and also the length of the track as well as the cars are too powerful in my opinion for that size of track as the cars won't be able to get a lot of speed."

Speaking on whether or not Mildenhall may be able to get its spot back on the F1 calendar, Andy reckons that, "If it does get enough interest regarding car numbers and spectators turning up to watch, it will regain a place for the F1s to race there again and it will get a couple more meetings each season as well."

Speaking on whether or not Mildenhall could fill the hole Coventry left, Andy was clear: "No! I can't see it filling the gap that Coventry had within the F1 community, again mainly due to the width and length of the track compared to Coventry as the racing would not be as fast and competitive as it was at Coventry."

It seems that not even the track commentator knows what to expect next April when the F1s make their eagerly anticipated return to the Suffolk shale venue. Hopefully it will be a great night irrespective of what car numbers are like. Perhaps the return of an old shale stadium can even go some way to halting the 'Coventry effect'.

Stuart Smith Junior celebrates his first major title since 2009

NATIONAL POINTS CHAMPIONSHIP SHOOTOUT

1. STUART SMITH JUNIOR (390)

2. Danny Wainman (212)
3. Nigel Green (445)

4. Frankie Wainman Junior (515) 5. Lee Fairhurst (217)
6. Mat Newson (16) 7. Ben Riley (422) 8. Paul Hines (259)
9. Craig Finnikin (55) 10. Ryan Harrison (197)
11. Dan Johnson (4) 12. Luke Davidson (464)

Words: Rhosanna Jenkins
Photos: Colin Casserley

Fought over ten rounds – starting at Birmingham Wheels on 26 August and culminating in the double points finale at Belle Vue on 12 November – the 2017 Shootout for the silver roof again went down to the wire, numerically speaking, but was really all about one driver setting out his stall early on and leaving the other eleven to play catch up. The Shootout was originally designed to add some intensity and action to the tail end of the season. 2017 was pretty much devoid of a silver top around the tracks, as the 2016 champion, Rob Speak, retired at the end of last season to become the promoter of Skegness Stadium.

The twelve drivers who progressed to the Mintex National Points Championship Shootout, in bonus point order (two points for each meeting attended and an extra point for each final win) were: Frankie Wainman Junior, Ben Riley, Mat Newson, Danny Wainman, Nigel Green, Stuart Smith Junior, Paul Hines, Craig Finnikin, Lee Fairhurst, Dan Johnson, Luke Davidson and Ryan Harrison.

Out of the twelve contenders, only four had previously held the silver roof. The World Champion, Nigel Green, was only competing in his second Shootout, but he'd come very close to winning it in his first year and was clearly on form this year, so no one could bet against him. Ben Riley was a newcomer to the Shootout, making it into the top twelve for the first time. Competing in the Shootout was one of

Seven of the Shootout contenders made it to the last round at Belle Vue

Ryan Harrison shot to the top of the leaderboard after round one

Riley's racing goals and it was great to see him achieve it. Riley is from a racing family and it is easy to forget that he is only in his third season in the F1s.

After Tom Harris' racing ban, Paul Hines was promoted to become the twelfth driver in the race for the silver. Although not expecting to be in the 2017 competition, Hines is no stranger to the Shootout. He's competed several times and even finished third in 2010. As well as Harris, another notable exception to this year's Shootout was Mick Sworder. Mick had missed shale racing for much of the season after blowing an engine early on, and then suffered injury and a subsequent ban after the incident with Tom Harris.

With the 12 drivers designated, fans were all set for a captivating and dramatic title battle. The opening round of the Shootout, held at Birmingham Wheels in August, saw Ryan Harrison climb from the bottom of the points table all of the way to the top. Stuart Smith Junior's second place in the final and Grand National victory brought him up to second place. Dan Johnson had slipped to last spot just below Craig Finnikin (both absent from Birmingham).

Two days later, at the *Stock Car Magazine* sponsored round 2 at Belle Vue, Stuart Smith Junior followed up a second place in his heat with a final win, taking the lead from Johnson with one to go. Going into the round, Smith was four points behind Harrison. By the end of the meeting, Smith had a healthy 25-point lead from Frankie Wainman Junior second and Nigel Green third.

After a break for the World Final, the Shootout continued three weeks later, at King's Lynn on 23 September. The Bensons Products Ltd round 3 saw a heat and final double plus a fourth place in the Grand National for Stuart Smith Junior. The 390 driver entered the round 25 points ahead of 515 and 445, and by the end of the night, his lead had extended to 40 points. Second-placed man, FWJ, had a good night, as did Danny Wainman, who was able to have a brief stint in the third spot in the Shootout standings.

A two-thirds format was adopted for round 4 at Owlerton Stadium in Sheffield, so full Shootout points were not awarded, but that certainly didn't stop certain drivers getting stuck in. The final was won by Craig Finnikin after points leader Smith and British Champion Frankie Wainman Junior clashed. Finnikin was the highest points scorer, but after missing earlier rounds, was never really in contention for the silver.

Three Shootout drivers (4, 464 and 197) didn't make it to Belle Vue for Shootout round 5, which was run by Coventry Stox and saw Lee Fairhurst romp away with the final. Despite not scoring as highly in the Richard Baldwin Motorhomes-sponsored round, it was clear by this stage that Stuart Smith Junior was the favourite to win the

Davidson, Riley and Fairhurst take to shale in round 2

Ryan Harrison decorated the Skegness tarmac with rubber, but SSJ was close behind

silver. At this half way stage, Smith was 47 points ahead of Fairhurst in second and Newson in third.

Back to the tarmac for round 6 at Skegness, which was sponsored by J Davidson Scrap Metal Processors, and it was a return to form for Ryan Harrison. Despite getting off to a good start Ryan Harrison was unable to attend rounds three to five, so he dropped down the points table. Given his performance in the other rounds, if he'd attended all of them, Ryan could have been a serious challenger for the silver. The 197 pilot was the highest Shootout finisher in his heat and took the final victory after a last-bend move on long-time leader Randall. Unfortunately for Harrison, Smith was right behind him, so he couldn't gain on the points leader. Fairhurst was still hanging on in second position, with FWJ back up to third in the standings.

The next stop on the Shootout calendar was back to the Adrian Flux Arena in King's Lynn for round 7 and Smith continued to dominate. Sponsored by Neil Stuchbury Motors, it was a typical King's Lynn action-packed meeting, benefitting from the addition of a number of Dutch drivers. A heat win and second place in the final boosted Nigel Green's points total but Smith's second place in the Grand National turned the screw just that little bit tighter.

American Racer-sponsored round 8 at Birmingham Wheels saw a continuation of good form for both Ryan Harrison and Stuart Smith Junior. Harrison took the flag and another Birmingham victory, while Smith finished in seventh. Nigel Green was continuing to stay out of trouble and bank some points and by the end of the night had moved up to third in the Shootout points table.

The following day it was off to Northampton for the penultimate round, which was sponsored by Teng Tools. After picking up the first win of the day, Nigel Green went on to claim his eleventh final win of the season, but his first of the Shootout. This was glimmer of hope and pushed Green into second place, but he was still an unbelievable 119 points behind Smith.

Into the final round and with double the points on offer, there was only the one driver who could mathematically take the silver roof away from Stuart Smith Junior – but this would have involved Smith not finishing at all and Green scoring extremely well. Green must have known it was the longest of long shots and, in the end, not even the World and European Champion could stop the Rochdale super-star. Stuart continued his winning ways at Belle Vue, crossing the line first in both heats. The team had a silver wing ready and waiting to adorn the car in the meeting final.

Frankie Wainman Junior continues to look for his first Shootout win – he eventually claimed fourth place in 2017

The Shootout top three, including a career-best second place for Danny Wainman

SSJ last won the silver roof in 2009, when the Shootout was still being developed, a victory that was his last major championship win. He failed to qualify for the 2016 Shootout but definitely dominated 2017. Smith ended the series on 338 points, 142 ahead of the rest of the contenders. What was more interesting was the three-way battle for second place. In the end, only four points covered second to fifth positions. Danny Wainman was one point ahead of Nigel Green, who had Frankie Wainman Junior one point behind him. Lee Fairhurst finished a further two points back in fifth place. First-timer Riley finished in seventh.

Stuart Smith Junior consistently scored, racking up the points in every round. He won three finals, three heats and one Grand National throughout the Shootout. He finished on the podium in six of the ten rounds. It was the most comprehensive victory in the history of the Shootout and Stuart Smith Junior will certainly deserve to sport the silver roof throughout 2018.

Whilst maybe not as lively as previous years, the Shootout still bought some spark of the end of the season. Originally, the Shootout series was brought in to mirror the NASCAR style, but now that NASCAR has changed, will BriSCA follow suit? On the other hand, as the saying goes, 'if it ain't broke...'

2017 was a career best season for Nigel Green,
and hopefully not his last

DRIVER OF THE YEAR

NIGEL GREEN

The Driver of the Year is chosen by the F1stockcars.com editorial team.

Previous winner of the award:
2016 Frankie Wainman Junior

Words: Scott Reeves
Photos: Colin Casserley

The arrival of a relatively new surname at the top table of Formula 1 stock car racing is an increasingly rare thing and something to be celebrated – although it should be pointed out that the Green family was not unknown to the motorsport world before Nigel strapped himself in the cab of his Formula 1 stock car. Father Roger raced F1 for a couple of years in the 1990s, while brother Jamie spent a few seasons in Ministox before switching to karting. Jamie's obvious talent saw him climb the circuit racing ladder, eventually landing in the German Touring Car Championship, where he has claimed three series podiums in thirteen years of racing.

Nigel's own experiences behind the wheel began on the Isle of Man at the tender age of nine, where he raced his Ministox into a fence post in his only meeting in the formula. Then he followed his brother into karting, although Nigel lacked the same passion Jamie showed for the circuits and began to cast his eye further afield for his racing fix.

Enter Mick Sworder. Unbeknown to Mr Box Office at the time, it was seeing Mick drive with the Formula 2 gold roof at Birmingham that inspired Nigel to return to the ovals. With only one meeting under his belt, and that at the age of nine, Nigel was certainly jumping in at the deep end, yet his natural gift for racing shone through. He

Green smokes his tyres after taking his first major title — the 2017 European Championship...

...but the red and yellow was only on display for a couple of months

won his first race, fittingly at Birmingham, the place he decided to buy a Formula 2.

Over six seasons between 2008 and 2013, Nigel was well known as a talented F2 red top, albeit one who didn't usually take the chequered flag at championship events. Second place in the 2009 European Championship was the closest he came to big success, although he did manage to take two Shootout titles on the trot in 2012 and 2013 (a time when the F2 version of the Shootout was a single race held at the last meeting of the season).

Eventually, the lure of racing at the pinnacle of oval motorsport drew too strong. Nigel wanted to race in front of big crowds, but he also wanted to challenge for big championships. If he was going to switch from F2 to F1, he was going to do it properly. He invested in Andy Smith's old tarmac car, the 2008 World Final winner, and two shale cars from the Murray Harrison stable.

So it was that Nigel Green rolled out on track in F1 445 for the first time at the end of 2014. Racing under a blue roof courtesy of his prior experience, he earned a race win before the end of the year. 2015 was a season in which he found his feet, steadily climbing the grading list and claiming a red roof. By 2016, he was racing under the flashing lights of a superstar and a first championship trophy seemed to be a question of when, not if.

Fast-forward to the 2017 European Championship. Using a new qualification system, which saw the grid for the championship race decided by an aggregate of points over the weekend, Nigel claimed the outside of the front row. No disrespect to Scott Davids, the driver in pole position, but the result was never really in doubt. Using his superior hardware, Nigel drove off into the sunset to take a deserved first title.

Nor was it a one-off. Nigel took the chequered flag 22 times over the course of the season, a whopping 11 of which were meeting finals. That saw him comfortably top the World Championship qualifying table and select pole position for the Skegness semi-final. If nobody got to him on the first corner, there was little doubt that Nigel would drive off for an easy win again. They didn't, and he did.

Surely in the World Final, somebody would take the bull by the horns and try to take out the overwhelming favourite on the first corner? Nope. Although no World Final winner would ever say that winning the biggest race of the season was easy, the truth is that Nigel wasn't particularly tested on his way to victory in 2017.

Why? Part of the explanation is that Nigel was the dominant man on tarmac. The Andy Smith car that won the 2008 World Final at Ipswich was the same one Nigel used to win the 2017 World Final at Ipswich, although it was all but unrecognisable. Nigel took the brave

Team Green celebrate winning the World Final

Gold and silver clashed almost straight away after Stuart Smith Junior took the National Points title

step of cutting up a proven race winner owned by a legend of the sport, rebuilding it with new suspension, engine and axles – more on that later.

Since Nigel started the season saying that his main goal was to win the silver roof, perhaps he considers 2017 to have been a failure – after all, he finished third in that particular series! Yet in all seriousness, Nigel completed the season as World and European Champion and the new dominant force in the sport. There's little doubt he was the driver of the year.

The next question is: how do you beat Nigel Green? According to some, the only way to do it is to ban his car. The radical redesign of the ex-Andy Smith machine fell foul of the BSCDA at their AGM in January 2018, which banned rear axles beyond a certain width. Nigel left that meeting aggrieved, feeling singled out and aware that another rebuild would be required to get his car back on the pace.

As a result, the chances are we might see the European and World Champion much less next year, if at all. That would be a real shame. Some may not agree with the direction he is taking the sport, but even those who oppose the width of his rear must admit that he is an intelligent, talented and sharp racing driver. Nigel Green has been a breath of fresh air in a season which could have been stale after the loss of Coventry – let's hope he comes back, and hungry for more.

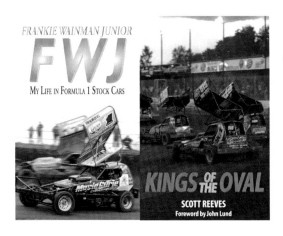

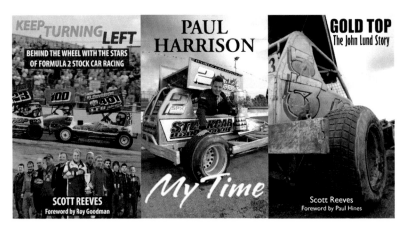